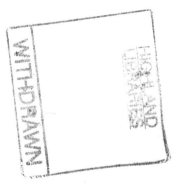

EXPLORING THE SOLAR SYSTEM

URANUS, NEPTUNE & PLUTO

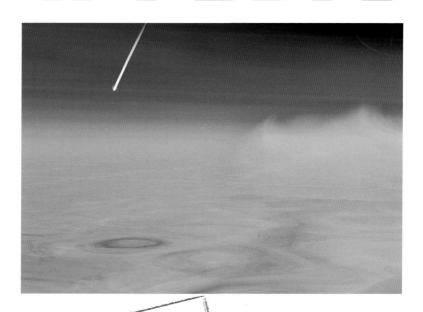

GILES SPARROW

Heinemann
LIBRARY

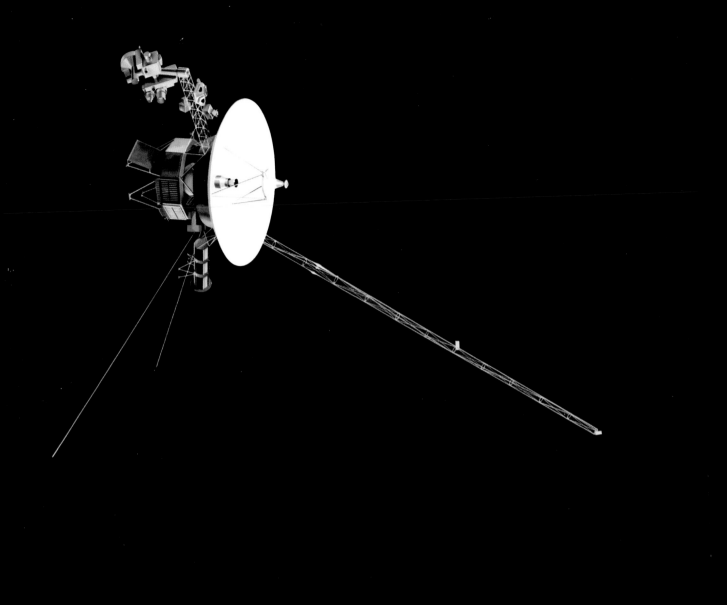

URANUS, NEPTUNE & PLUTO

Published by Heinemann Library,
a division of Reed Educational & Professional Publishing,
Halley Court, Jordan Hill,
Oxford OX2 8EJ, UK
Visit our website at www.heinemann.co.uk/library

Produced by Brown Partworks
Project Editor: Ben Morgan
Deputy Editor: Sally McFall
Managing Editor: Anne O'Daly
Designer: Michael LeBihan
Illustrator: Mark Walker
Picture Researcher: Helen Simm
Consultant: Peter Bond

© 2001 Brown Partworks Limited

Printed in Singapore

ISBN 0 431 12265 2 (hardback)   ISBN 0 431 12274 1 (paperback)
06 05 04 03 02 01   06 05 04 03 02 01
10 9 8 7 6 5 4 3 2 1   10 9 8 7 6 5 4 3 2 1

British Library Cataloguing in Publication Data

Sparrow, Giles
   Uranus, Neptune & Pluto. – (Exploring the solar system)
   1.Uranus, Neptune & Pluto – Juvenile literature
   I.Title
   523.4

BELOW: *The planets of the Solar System, shown in order from the Sun:
Mercury, Venus, Earth, Mars, Jupiter, Saturn, Uranus, Neptune, Pluto.*

CONTENTS

*Some words are shown in bold, **like this**.*
You can find out what they mean by looking in the glossary.

where are the outer planets?

Uranus, Neptune and Pluto are the furthest of the Solar System's nine planets, and they are sometimes called the outer planets. Like all the planets, they are trapped by the Sun's powerful **gravity** and travel around the Sun along paths called **orbits**. Their orbits are far out in the depths of space, where the Sun is little more than a bright star.

Uranus is the seventh planet from the Sun. It is 19 times further out than Earth, so it takes much longer than Earth to orbit the Sun. Uranus's year – the time it takes to orbit the Sun once – lasts 84 Earth years. Between our planet and Uranus lie Mars, the **asteroid belt** and the gigantic planets Jupiter and Saturn.

Neptune is even further away, orbiting the Sun once every 164 Earth years at an average distance of 4.5 billion kilometres (2.8 billion miles). Uranus and Neptune are like twins. They are similar in colour, the same size and made of the same materials. Both are **gas giants** – huge planets made up mostly of **hydrogen**.

Getting to Uranus

The time it takes to get to Uranus depends on how you travel. These figures assume you travel in a straight line at a constant speed, but in reality it would take longer.

Distance from Earth to Uranus
Closest   2.7 billion km
           (1.7 billion miles)
Furthest   3 billion km
           (1.9 billion miles)

**By car at 113 km per hour
(70 miles per hour)**
Closest   2770 years
Furthest   3100 years

**By rocket at 11 km per second
(7 miles per second)**
Closest   7 years 8 months
Furthest   8 years 7 months

Time for radio signals to reach Uranus (at the speed of light)
Closest   2 hours 32 minutes
Furthest   2 hours 47 minutes

Distance from the Sun

The diagram shows how incredibly far the outer planets are. Neptune and Pluto are too far to see with the naked eye, but Uranus is just visible if you know where to look.

Sun Mercury Venus Earth Mars Jupiter Saturn

0   1000 (621)   2000 (1243)
Distance in millions of kilometres (millions of miles)

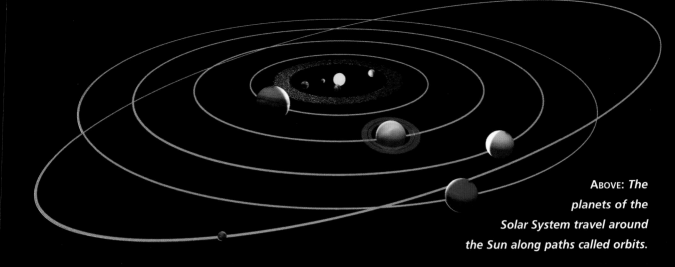

ABOVE: *The planets of the Solar System travel around the Sun along paths called orbits.*

Uranus and Neptune are enormous – each could swallow Earth's volume more than 50 times over. Yet they are much smaller than the gas giants Jupiter and Saturn, the true kings of the Solar System.

Pluto is usually the furthest planet, but its strange orbit sometimes takes it closer to the Sun than Neptune. Pluto's orbit is an **ellipse** – a stretched circle. As a result, the planet's distance from the Sun varies from 4.5 billion kilometres (2.8 billion miles) to more than 7.5 billion kilometres (4.6 billion miles). Pluto also has a much more tilted orbit than most planets, taking it above and below the plane of the Solar System. Because Pluto is so far out it has the longest year of any planet, taking a staggering 248 Earth years to complete just one orbit around the Sun. It spends just 20 Earth years of its orbit closer to the Sun than Neptune. Unlike the other outer planets, Pluto is tiny. In fact, it is only about two-thirds as wide as Earth's moon.

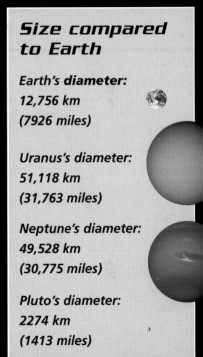

Size compared to Earth

Earth's diameter:
12,756 km
(7926 miles)

Uranus's diameter:
51,118 km
(31,763 miles)

Neptune's diameter:
49,528 km
(30,775 miles)

Pluto's diameter:
2274 km
(1413 miles)

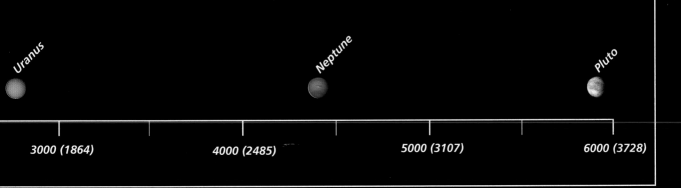

Uranus   Neptune   Pluto

3000 (1864)   4000 (2485)   5000 (3107)   6000 (3728)

First view

Imagine you're going on a **mission** to Uranus, Neptune and Pluto. Before setting off you decide to look at the planets from Earth, but this is far from easy. Uranus, the closest and brightest of the three planets, is just a faint green 'star' to the naked eye. Neptune and Pluto can only be seen with powerful telescopes.

Photographs taken by the Hubble Space Telescope and other observatories reveal more, showing that Uranus and Neptune are both turquoise. Uranus is a little greener, and Neptune a little bluer. But Pluto just looks like a smudge, even through the Hubble Space Telescope. The only way to tell that it is a planet is to plot its movements by taking two photographs a few days apart. Stars stay in the same position relative to each other, but planets are always on the move.

ABOVE: *Pluto (top) and its moon Charon (bottom) look like smudges even through the Hubble Space Telescope.*

It's time to set off. Your spaceship has been fitted with an engine that will burn slowly for years, steadily increasing your speed. Even so, the journey will take a lifetime because the distances involved are colossal. The only way to survive the trip is to go into **suspended animation** – a state like hibernation, in which your body is preserved by extreme cold and chemicals. Scientists do not yet know how to put people into suspended animation, so we will imagine that your trip to the outer Solar System takes place some time in the future when the technology has been perfected.

*To save fuel, the first stage of your trip to the outer planets takes place on a space shuttle. The shuttle ferries you to an interplanetary spacecraft waiting in **orbit** around Earth.*

Getting closer

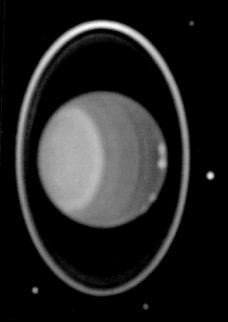

ABOVE: *This false-colour picture from the Hubble Space Telescope shows Uranus's unusual tilt and its **rings**. The grey blobs are Uranian moons.*

RIGHT: *The* Voyager 2 ***space probe** took this spectacular picture of a **crescent** Uranus as it flew past the planet in January 1986.*

After travelling for fifteen years, you are woken by the ship's computers. Uranus is straight ahead. It looks about the size of the Moon from Earth, but it is much paler because sunlight is weak this far out in the Solar System.

You carefully examine the planet for any kind of detail on the surface, but you can't see a thing. Uranus is as smooth and featureless as an egg, with no sign of solid ground visible through the blue-green **atmosphere.** Uranus is probably a slushy mixture of gas and liquid, like the larger **gas giants** Jupiter and Saturn. Unlike Jupiter and Saturn, though, it doesn't show any visible sign of stormy weather or wind in its atmosphere.

Soon you notice several moons orbiting Uranus, but there's something strange. Instead of disappearing behind Uranus as they orbit, the moons rise over it and then sink below, performing cartwheels around the planet. Moons usually orbit around a planet's **equator**, so could Uranus be tipped on its side? You check your instruments and there's no mistake – Uranus is tipped right over, with one **pole** facing the Sun. As a result, the Uranus system rolls along as it orbits the Sun, instead of spinning like a top as other planets do.

Close encounter

Uranus is now close enough and bright enough to see a little detail in its **atmosphere**. By using a red filter to block out blue and green light, you can see faint bands of clouds around the planet and a pinkish haze around its edge, visible against the blackness of space.

Your flight path takes you very close to Uranus. As you hurtle towards the planet, you notice a thin shadow stretching across the surface in a straight line. Looking up, you see that the Sun is flickering as something passes over its face. The only explanation is that Uranus has **rings**, though they must be much fainter and smaller than the magnificent rings of Saturn.

ABOVE: *Uranus's blue-green atmosphere makes the planet look bland and featureless, even from up close.*

Even though you're now speeding over the upper atmosphere, Uranus is still remarkably plain. But the stillness is deceptive – your instruments reveal that strong winds are blowing around the planet at up to 580 kilometres per hour (360 miles per hour). The temperature in the upper atmosphere is –214°C (–350°F). This seems to be the same across the whole planet, from the daylit to the dark side.

BELOW: *A meteor burns up as it enters Uranus's atmosphere in this artist's impression.*

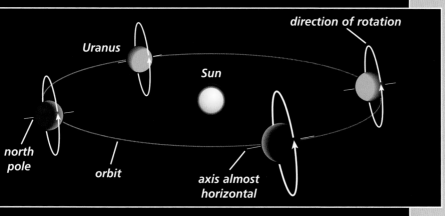

Uranus

direction of rotation

Sun

north
pole

orbit

axis almost
horizontal

*Uranus's tilt gives the planet very strange days and years. Uranus's year – the time it takes to **orbit** the Sun – lasts 84 Earth years. For roughly half of each orbit, the north pole receives constant sunlight and it is summer north of the **equator**. This is followed by a 42-year winter, with the north plunged into permanent night as it points away from the Sun. The length of a day, measured from one sunrise to the next, depends on where you are on Uranus. At the poles, a day from sunrise to sunrise lasts 84 Earth years, or one Uranian year. But near the equator, a day from sunrise to sunrise is seventeen hours – the same as a sidereal day.*

Because the surface of Uranus is almost featureless, it's difficult to see how quickly the planet **rotates**. However, your ship's instruments can detect Uranus's **magnetic field**, which rotates along with the planet. It turns out that Uranus rotates once every seventeen hours – the length of its **sidereal day**.

You discover something unusual about Uranus's magnetic field. In most planets the magnetic field lines up roughly with the planet's **axis**, so the **magnetic poles** are close to the **north pole** and **south pole**. But on Uranus the field is tilted at an angle of 60 degrees. Even stranger, the magnetic field does not even pass through the centre of Uranus. You wonder what could have caused the planet's unusual tilt and magnetism.

William Herschel (1738–1822)

*William Herschel was a German musician who escaped from Germany during a war with France and settled in England. He was an enthusiastic amateur astronomer and built his own telescopes to study the skies from his garden. His telescopes, designed to look at distant stars and **nebulas**, were the best in the world. In 1781 Herschel discovered Uranus – the first new planet to be found for thousands of years. The discovery made him famous, and he became King George III's personal astronomer.*

Uranus's rings

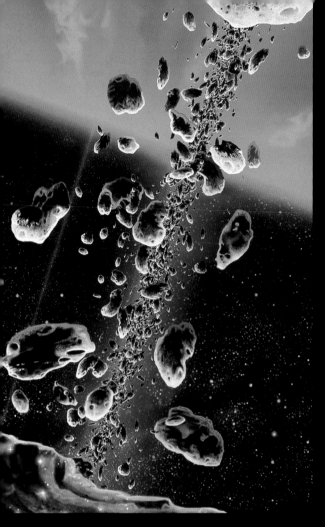

You swing the ship away from the surface of Uranus to take a closer look at the planet's **rings**. But this is easier said than done. Although you can see the rings silhouetted against the planet, they are so dark that they disappear against the blackness of space. However, your ship's **radar** shows them clearly and allows you to chart a course through them.

Like Saturn's rings, the rings around Uranus are divided into lots of separate rings. Each ring is made up of millions of individual objects that average about 1 metre (3 feet) wide and **orbit** the planet together. As you swoop between the rings, you launch a **space probe** to analyse these mysterious objects. The probe's chemical sniffers reveal that the objects are blocks of frozen **methane**. By contrast, Saturn's rings are made of chunks of ice. Perhaps this is why Saturn's rings are so much brighter.

ABOVE: *The rings around Uranus, shown in this artist's impression, are made of millions of chunks of frozen methane.*

Astronomers discovered the rings around Uranus by accident. In 1977 they were watching Uranus pass in front of a star. This allowed them to measure the planet's size and shape accurately, and the way the star's light faded as it disappeared gave clues about Uranus's **atmosphere**. But everyone was surprised when the star flickered several times as it got close to the planet. The astronomers soon realized that the flickering was caused by the star passing behind a series of thin rings.

The bright lines crossing this image are the rings of Uranus, revealed in false colour by the Voyager 2 *space probe. Uranus has at least nine rings.*

Landing on Miranda

Before leaving the Uranus system to set off for Neptune, you decide to take a quick tour of Uranus's moons. First on the list is Miranda, a 480-kilometre-wide (300-mile-wide) moon that turns out to be one of the weirdest worlds in the Solar System. Miranda's surface is a crazy patchwork of different landscapes that don't match each other. Something amazing must have happened to this little moon in the distant past.

You land on top of some tall cliffs and step outside. You're only one-fortieth of your Earth weight in Miranda's weak **gravity**, which makes it difficult to balance as you move. In one direction lies a plain covered with **impact craters**, and in the other direction is a buckled landscape covered with ridges. The cliff you're on forms the boundary between the two landscapes.

Miranda probably once had craters all over, so what process could have covered part of it with ridges? And why is there such a dramatic boundary between the two landscapes? It's as if the moon was broken apart and put back together in a jumble. Perhaps you'll find more clues to this mystery by visiting Uranus's other moons. Before you leave, you dig up a sample of Miranda's surface rock to analyse back on board. The sample turns out to be a mixture of rock, ice and frozen methane. The upper surface is darkened by the frozen methane, but the icy mixture beneath this is bright.

Miranda's bizarre surface is twisted and stretched into all kinds of strange patterns – a clue that something violent happened in this moon's history.

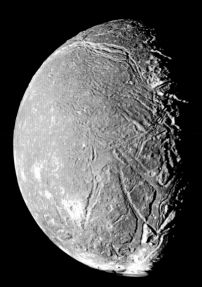

ABOVE: *Ariel is a maze of canyons and ridges. The canyons have flat floors where they filled with molten materials that froze.*

Uranus has eighteen named moons and several unnamed ones – more than any other planet in the Solar System. Most are less than 80 kilometres (50 miles) wide, but five are much larger. These are known as the major moons.

In order from Uranus, the major moons are Miranda, Ariel, Umbriel, Titania and Oberon. Ariel and Umbriel are both around 1170 kilometres (730 miles) across, while Titania and Oberon are both about 1550 kilometres (960 miles) wide – just less than half the width of Earth's moon. All the moons have dark surfaces, so you can only see detail from close up.

Umbriel is the most crater-covered of the Uranian moons. This faint picture was taken by the Voyager 2 *space probe.*

Ariel is the brightest. As you fly past you see that, like Miranda, Ariel has had a very active past. Deep canyons divide the surface up into blocks. The bottoms of these canyons are flat – perhaps they were once flooded with molten rock or slushy ice that froze completely solid.

Next you arrive at Umbriel. This battered world is covered with **impact craters** – far more than on Ariel or Miranda. There are a few canyons, but even these have been cratered over. The number of craters suggests that Umbriel's surface is very old.

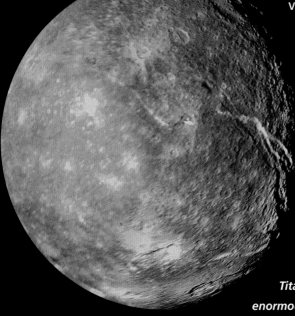

Titania is peppered with many small craters and a few enormous ones. It also has deep canyons like those on Ariel.

Further out from Uranus you pass Titania and Oberon. These moons are also heavily cratered, but less so than Umbriel. Both also have canyons like those on Ariel. Here and there, the craters are surrounded by bright splashes – icy material thrown across the surface by the violent collisions that formed the craters.

Oberon's biggest craters are surrounded by bright splashes where ice has been gouged out from the moon's interior. This image from Voyager 2 also shows a mountain 6 kilometres (4 miles) tall on the lower left horizon.

Titania, Oberon and Umbriel follow a simple rule: the larger a planet or moon is, the more active its history. Large worlds hold more heat inside, which can cause molten rock and ice to erupt onto the surface and cover craters. Titania and Oberon are the largest moons, so they have fewer craters than Umbriel, as you would expect. But Ariel and Miranda are small, yet they have few craters and show signs of an active history. Astronomers once thought Miranda might have been smashed by a collision and then been brought back together by **gravity**. However, most astronomers now think that another force could explain its jumbled surface. Miranda and Ariel are both caught in a tug of war between the gravity of Uranus and that of the other moons, and this made them heat up. Miranda got so hot that some areas of **crust** sank down and were covered over. Ariel swelled with heat and then shrank as it cooled, producing canyons where its surface cracked.

Ten years after leaving Uranus, you wake up from **suspended animation** in time for your arrival at Neptune. The dimly lit blue planet looms out of the darkness ahead. Neptune is so far out in the Solar System that it receives less than half as much sunlight as Uranus.

Even from a distance you can see that Neptune is different from Uranus, despite being a similar size and colour. The most striking difference is that Neptune's weather is very violent. The planet has dark and light cloud bands that remind you of Jupiter's stripes. And you can see right away that Neptune is not toppled over like Uranus. It is tilted at 28 degrees from vertical – almost the same as Earth's tilt.

Neptune's dark spots are storms the size of Earth. The storms on Neptune have much shorter lives than Jupiter's famous Great Red Spot. Neptune's 'Great Dark Spot', shown in the Voyager 2 *picture below, faded away over several years as it tried to cross the planet's equator.*

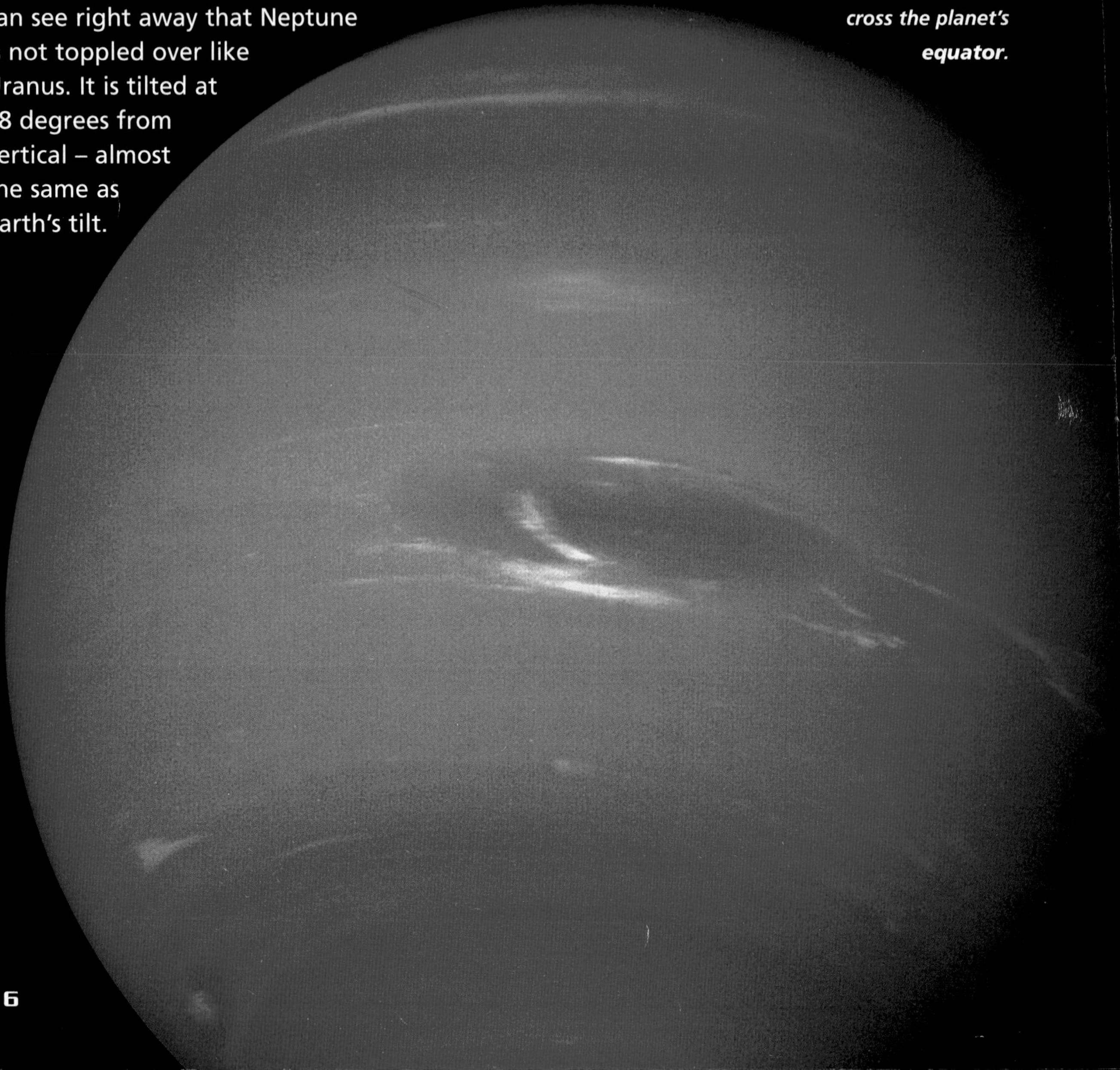

Ferocious winds blow Neptune's clouds into long streaks. The white clouds in this Voyager 2 image have cast shadows on the blue clouds below.

The most striking feature on Neptune is a large dark spot near the equator. This is actually a gigantic storm, similar to Jupiter's **Great Red Spot**. Elsewhere, bright white clouds stretch around the planet, blown into streaks by high winds. They remind you of the high **cirrus** clouds that sometimes appear on Earth during fine weather. You can just see long shadows cast by the clouds on the darker blue cloud layers below. The high clouds probably occur where warm air is rising through colder surroundings. Although Neptune receives less heat from the Sun than Uranus does, its upper **atmosphere** is about the same temperature, at −214°C (−350°F).

As you get close to the planet, you measure the wind speed in the upper atmosphere. The wind turns out to be much stronger than on Uranus, reaching up to 2000 kilometres per hour (1250 miles per hour). This makes Neptune the windiest planet in the Solar System! The winds seem to get faster higher up. The fastest-moving clouds on the planet are small white 'scooters' that circle Neptune in 78 hours.

As at Uranus, you can measure the length of Neptune's **sidereal day** by monitoring its **magnetic field**. Neptune has a sidereal day of 16 hours, and this closely matches its daylength from sunrise to sunrise. Like that of Uranus, Neptune's magnetic field is tilted away from the **poles**. If Earth's magnetic field were tilted as much, our planet's north **magnetic pole** would be as far away from the true **north pole** as Chicago or Rome.

Getting to Neptune

The time it takes to reach Neptune depends on how you travel. These figures assume you travel in a straight line at a constant speed, but in reality it would take longer.

Distance from Earth to Neptune
Closest   **4.3 billion km**
              (2.7 billion miles)
Furthest   **4.7 billion km**
              (2.9 billion miles)

By car at 113 km per hour
(70 miles per hour)
Closest   **4400 years**
Furthest   **4730 years**

By rocket at 11 km per second
(7 miles per second)
Closest   **12 years 3 months**
Furthest   **13 years 2 months**

Time for radio signals to reach Neptune (at the speed of light)
Closest   **4 hours 8 minutes**
Furthest   **4 hours 12 minutes**

Moons and rings

Neptune has a family of eight moons and, like Uranus, several dark **rings**. As you skim across the rings you realize they are very strange – they are much thicker on one side of the planet than the other.

Soon you discover Neptune's small inner moons. These five moons are chunks of rock and ice up to 104 kilometres (65 miles) wide. Also called shepherd moons, they 'herd' the ring **particles** into tight circles with their **gravity**.

Beyond the shepherd moons are Neptune's three major moons: Proteus, Triton and Nereid. Proteus and Nereid are both small, dark, icy moons covered with craters – a bit like Uranus's moon Umbriel. You get a distant glimpse of Proteus as you fly past, but to see Nereid you have to look through a telescope. Nereid has a wildly stretched and tilted **orbit** around Neptune. At its furthest it is 10 million kilometres (6 million miles) from Neptune, but at its closest it is only 1.4 million kilometres (860,000 miles) away.

Now you're approaching Triton, Neptune's biggest moon. At 2710 kilometres (1680 miles) across, Triton is only slightly smaller than Earth's Moon and is far bigger than the rest of Neptune's moons put together. Triton orbits Neptune in an almost perfectly circular path, but it goes in the opposite direction from all the other moons. The closer you get to Triton, the more this moon seems out of place. It is much brighter than the other moons and it has hardly any craters, which means that its surface must have been covered over recently.

ABOVE: *Neptune's thin, dark rings are difficult to see. This photograph was taken by a very sensitive camera, with Neptune's glare blocked out in the middle. The rings are thicker on the left.*

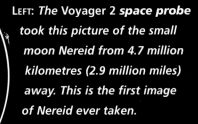

LEFT: *The* Voyager 2 *space probe took this picture of the small moon Nereid from 4.7 million kilometres (2.9 million miles) away. This is the first image of Nereid ever taken.*

Some parts of Triton are pink or blue-grey, so there must be several different types of chemical on the surface. Triton is much too interesting to pass by – you decide to land on the moon and explore. A quick check of your instruments reveals that the surface is hard enough to land on and that gravity is strong enough for walking.

BELOW: *Triton's varied and colourful surface is a contrast to Neptune's other, much smaller moons.*

Touchdown on Triton

You can see Triton's surface in great detail as you come in to land. Here and there, cracks run across the icy ground, and large areas are pitted with circular impressions like the surface of a cantaloup melon. Other regions have pushed up into hills, or formed smooth plains. There are also mysterious dark streaks where it looks as though soot has been daubed across the surface. Chemical sensors mounted on your **lander** reveal that Triton has a thin **atmosphere** made mostly of the gas nitrogen, with traces of **methane** and other gases.

Frost crunches under your feet as you step outside, but fortunately it's so cold that the ice is powder dry and not slippery. The temperature is −235°C (−391°F) – just 38°C (69°F) above absolute zero, the lowest temperature possible. Triton has more **gravity** than Miranda, but you're still only about one-tenth of your Earth weight. You've landed on a rolling, icy landscape, where a river of slush once flowed across the ground before freezing solid. Astronomers think Triton's interior may have been heated by the pull of Neptune's gravity, and this heating produced volcanoes that erupt slush instead of **lava**.

*This spectacular photograph of Triton shows the sooty streaks made by **geysers** (bottom) as well as pink and green frost made by frozen air (top). Triton is the coldest world in the Solar System.*

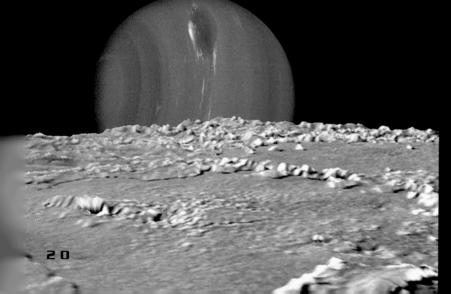

*The view from Triton might look like this 3-D reconstruction made from data sent to Earth by the Voyager 2 **space probe**. A vast frozen lake dominates Triton's surface in the foreground.*

Triton's seasons

The different colours on Triton, the frozen air and the geyser you saw are all linked to Triton's seasons. Triton's **orbit** combines with Neptune's to give the moon a 688-year cycle of seasons. Each **pole** receives hundreds of years of sunlight during its summer, followed by hundreds of years of freezing darkness in winter. During winter the thin air freezes on the ground and changes Triton's surface colour. In summer the frozen air evaporates, blows around Triton in the wind, and refreezes at the other pole. Some frozen air gets trapped underground and produces pockets of gas as it warms up. These burst out of the ground as geysers, throwing black dust into the air as they erupt. Earth's geysers (above right) are similar, but they are caused by heated water, not frozen air.

dust from geyser

You stoop down to collect a sample of ice, but suddenly the ground starts trembling and you fall over. Seconds later, a fountain of black dust and gas bursts out of a crack in the ground nearby and shoots up into the sky – a geyser. You can feel the ground shudder violently as the geyser erupts, but you can hear almost nothing because Triton's air is too thin to transmit sound. The geyser reaches a spectacular height in the low gravity, before blowing sideways in a gentle wind. Sooty dust grains begin to fall back to the ground, producing a dark streak across the landscape – just like the streaks you saw before landing.

The dimpled parts of Triton's surface are known as cantaloup terrain. Astronomers have yet to find out how this pattern formed.

It's time to return to your ship. After taking off from Triton's surface, you analyse the ice sample. Triton's **crust** mostly consists of a mixture of rock and ice. The surface of the ground is coated with a thin 'frost' made of frozen nitrogen, methane and carbon monoxide – the same chemicals that are found in Triton's atmosphere. Triton is so cold that its air freezes on the ground.

Inside Neptune and Uranus

As you prepare to leave the Neptune system and set off for Pluto, you puzzle over the two strange planets you've seen so far. Why is Uranus's weather so quiet while Neptune's is so violent? And why is Neptune the same temperature as Uranus when it's so much further from the Sun? The only explanation is that Neptune must have a source of heat inside it. You can measure how much heat is coming out of Neptune by using your ship's heat sensors. It turns out that the planet is pumping out an enormous amount of heat – twice as much as it receives from the Sun.

ocean

atmosphere

hot, slushy ice

rock core

If you could slice open Uranus and Neptune you would find that the two planets look similar inside. The outer **atmospheres** are mostly made of the lightweight gas **hydrogen**, along with **helium** and a small amount of **methane**. The methane gives both planets their blue-green colour. Neptune's atmosphere is about 3 per cent methane, while Uranus has only 2 per cent methane – that's why Neptune is bluer.

Uranus consists mostly of layers of gas, liquid and ice that merge together, with no definite boundaries. In the centre of the planet is a core of solid rock.

Deeper inside, the gases gradually turn to liquid as pressure pushes down on them. Roughly a quarter of the way in, the liquid layer gives way to a layer of slushy 'ice' made of water, ammonia and other heavy chemicals that have solidified and sunk towards the centre of the planet.

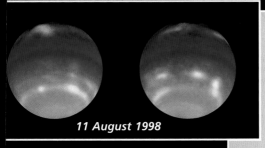

11 August 1998

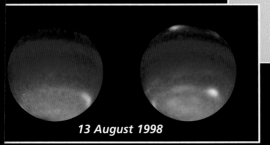

13 August 1998

Stormy Neptune

*Stormy weather on Earth is caused by the Sun's heat. Neptune's weather is stormier than Earth's, yet the Sun is 900 times dimmer, so astronomers think Neptune's weather must be driven by internal heat. These pictures, which combine images from the Hubble Space Telescope and a telescope in Hawaii, show just how quickly Neptune's atmosphere changes. The bright patches are clouds that move around the planet in bands parallel to the **equator**.*

This ice layer takes up most of each planet's volume – although Neptune and Uranus are called **gas giants**, they are really ice giants! Because the ice is squeezed tightly by **gravity**, it is very hot and partially molten. The constant swirling of this slushy layer creates the **magnetic field** of each planet.

At the centre of both Neptune and Uranus is a solid **core** of rock that contains most of each planet's **mass**. Uranus's core is about the size of Earth, but Neptune's is probably larger. Neptune's extra heat comes from within or around its core. Astronomers think the middle of the planet is shrinking due to gravity and producing heat as the pressure rises. Something similar happens inside Jupiter and Saturn. In fact, Uranus is the only gas giant that doesn't generate internal heat.

Neptune's interior is thought to be similar to Uranus's, but its core is larger.

ocean

atmosphere

hot, slushy ice

rock core

How Uranus and Neptune Formed

Uranus and Neptune both formed shortly after the Sun began to shine, roughly 4.5 billion years ago. The young Sun was surrounded by a vast cloud of gas and dust that eventually became the planets. The composition of this cloud varied with distance from the Sun. The planets of the inner Solar System are small and solid because the inner part of the cloud was mostly rock and metal. The outer part was rich in water and gases, which had been blown out of the inner Solar System by the Sun's energy. The **gas giant** planets – Jupiter, Saturn, Uranus and Neptune – formed largely from these materials.

Uranus and Neptune probably formed from the **core** outward. As dust particles in the cloud collided and stuck together, they grew into **planetesimals** – balls of rock with enough **gravity** to pull more material onto them.

The planets of the Solar System formed from a vast, disk-shaped cloud of gas and dust that surrounded the newborn Sun, as shown in this artist's impression. The gas giant planets, including Neptune and Uranus, formed in the outer part of the cloud.

Where did Triton come from?

Triton's strange, backward orbit gives the best clue to its origins, and also hints at why Neptune doesn't have as large a family of moons as the gas giants Jupiter, Saturn and Uranus. Astronomers think that Triton used to be a planet with its own orbit around the Sun, before a chance collision sent it hurtling towards Neptune. Neptune's gravity caught Triton and trapped it in a stretched, backward orbit. Over time, Neptune gradually pulled Triton into its circular orbit. Triton probably collided with Neptune's other moons, absorbing their material or flinging them out of the Neptune system. Proteus survived because it was very close to Neptune. Nereid also survived – but only just, which is why it has such a stretched orbit.

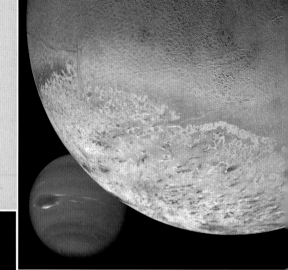

The planetesimals grew in size, sucking in **hydrogen** and **helium** from the cloud and developing huge **atmospheres**. They also pulled in ice and other frozen materials, which sank towards the centre of the growing planets and formed their slushy interiors. After the planets had formed they were still surrounded by a swirling disk of dust and ice, like a Solar System in miniature. This remaining material gradually condensed into moons.

Why are Uranus and Neptune smaller than the inner gas giants Jupiter and Saturn? Perhaps the answer is that they formed in the outer reaches of the Solar System, where the cloud of gas and dust that surrounded the young Sun contained less material.

The early history of the Solar System was violent. The young planets were often struck by planetesimals, **comets** and **asteroids**. One especially violent collision probably caused Uranus's unusual tilt by knocking the planet on its side. This seems to have happened long ago because Uranus's moons have since settled into stable **orbits**. Some astronomers think the collision that knocked Uranus over might somehow have caused the planet's strange lack of internal heat, but they are not sure how

Pluto and Charon

The journey to Pluto takes another twenty years. Although Pluto's **orbit** crosses Neptune's, the stretch and tilt of Pluto's path around the Sun mean that the two worlds never come close together. Sometimes they are a vast distance apart – if you'd set off at a different time the journey from Neptune to Pluto might have taken as long as 100 years!

Your ship's computer wakes you from **suspended animation** on your final approach to Pluto. You've been slowing down for the last leg of the journey so that you can use Pluto's **gravity** to swing the ship around and send you heading back to Earth. From a distance, Pluto looks like a ball of dark rock with a few brighter patches on the surface. It seems tiny after the giant worlds you've visited. Pluto is the smallest planet in the Solar System, and is actually smaller than many of the Solar System's moons, including Earth's moon.

ABOVE: *Pluto has distinct dark and light patches, as this artist's impression shows. The light patches are probably ice.*

Seeing Pluto

*No **space probes** have visited Pluto, so there are no clear photographs of its surface. Worse still, Pluto is so far away that trying to see detail on the planet is like trying to read the print on a golf ball 65 kilometres (40 miles) away. Even so, astronomers have managed to get a good look at Pluto. In the mid-1980s Charon's orbit took it directly in front of and behind Pluto. By measuring the change in brightness as Charon passed, astronomers built up crude maps of Pluto's surface. The images here, taken by the Hubble Space Telescope, show the front and back of Pluto in normal view (top) and enhanced by a computer (bottom).*

Charon is greyer than Pluto but shows similar bright and dark areas on its surface. This image is an artist's impression – no clear photographs of Charon exist.

As you get closer you notice a strange bulge on the top of the planet. After watching for a few hours you realize what it is – a huge moon rising from behind Pluto. This moon, called Charon, is over half the width of Pluto, yet its distance from Pluto is one-twentieth of the distance between Earth and our own moon. Like Pluto, Charon is covered in shiny patches. As it rises, you realize that the Pluto system, like Uranus, is tipped on its side.

Your ship's instruments tell you that Pluto and its single moon weigh very little, so they are probably mostly ice, mixed with a little rock. They are unlikely to have heavy metal **cores** like those found in Mercury, Venus, Earth and Mars.

Pluto looks a little like Neptune's moon Triton. There are faintly coloured patches of ice on the surface, and darker, reddish areas between the ice patches. The different colours indicate that there are several different chemicals frozen onto the ground. By analysing these colours you identify the chemicals nitrogen, **methane** and carbon monoxide – similar to the different ices on Triton. Surprisingly, Charon seems to have much more ice than Pluto, and it is greyer in colour. Despite these differences, astronomers think Charon formed from a chunk of Pluto that was blasted off the planet by a violent collision. Earth's own moon may have formed in the same way.

Getting to Pluto

The time it takes to reach Pluto depends on how you travel. These figures assume you could travel in a straight line at a constant speed, but in reality it would take longer.

Distance from Earth to Pluto
Closest   4.3 billion km
           (2.7 billion miles)
Furthest   7.6 billion km
           (4.7 billion miles)

By car at 70 miles per hour (113 km per hour)
Closest   4400 years
Furthest   7660 years

By rocket at 11 km per second (7 miles per second)
Closest   12 years 8 months
Furthest   21 years 3 months

Time for radio signals to reach Pluto (at the speed of light)
Closest   4 hours 7 minutes
Furthest   6 hours 58 minutes

A day on Pluto

You touch down on Pluto's daylit side and step out onto the icy surface. In the weak **gravity** you weigh about seven per cent of your Earth weight, so you have to wear heavy boots and a special belt to weigh you down. You also have to carry a torch because the Sun is just a bright star from Pluto, and daytime is as dark as a moonlit night on Earth. Pluto's surface is –230°C (–382°F) – almost as cold as Triton – but your thick spacesuit keeps you warm. The moon Charon hangs in the sky, a spectacular **crescent**. It looks amazingly large – more than seven times the size of a full moon seen from Earth.

Pluto's day is 6.4 Earth days long, the same time that Charon takes to **orbit** the planet. As a result, Charon never moves across Pluto's sky – from one side of Pluto you would never even know Charon was there! Pluto is the only planet that is locked facing its moon in this way. Charon also has one side permanently facing Pluto, and for this reason many astronomers call Pluto and Charon a double planet.

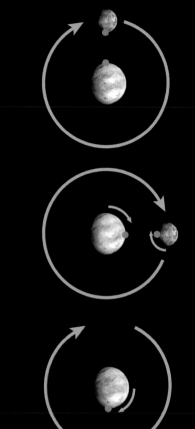

RIGHT: *Although Charon rotates as it orbits Pluto, the two worlds keep the same side facing each other all the time.*

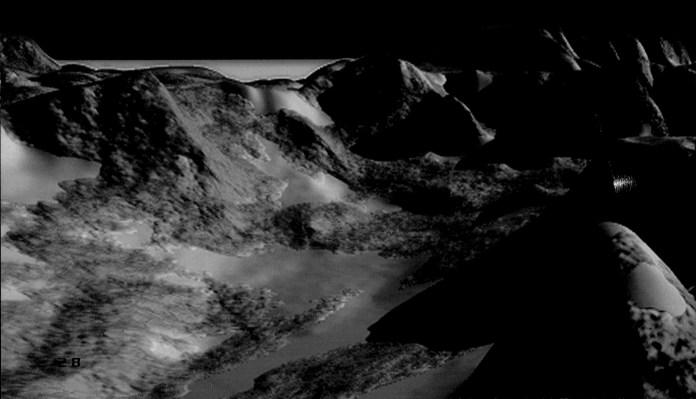

Astronomers puzzled over these strange movements for years until two mathematicians realized that they might be caused by the gravity of another planet beyond Uranus. The British mathematician John Couch Adams was first to make the calculations in 1843, but British astronomers refused to take his theory seriously. Frenchman Urbain Leverrier made the same calculations in 1846 and sent his results to Johann Gottfried Galle, a German astronomer at the Berlin Observatory, almost immediately. Galle saw Neptune on the night after receiving Leverrier's letter, and so became the first person to recognize the planet. Neptune was soon named after the Roman god of the sea because of its vivid blue colour.

Neptune was the Roman god of water and the sea. He is often depicted holding a three-pronged spear, or trident, which he used to create storms.

Pluto and Planet X

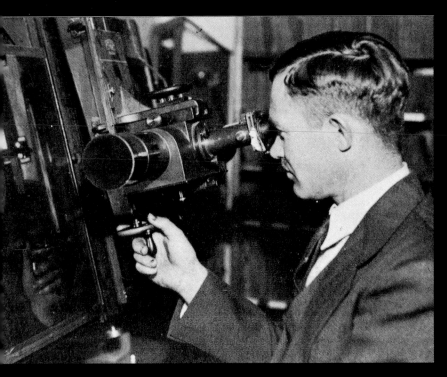

Pluto was discovered by the astronomer Clyde Tombaugh after months of painstaking searching.

In the late 1800s Neptune was the furthest known planet, but astronomers suspected there might be another planet beyond it. Neptune did not follow its predicted **orbit** – a sign that **gravity** from another planet was disturbing it. The US astronomer Percival Lowell even calculated the unknown planet's position, though he could not see it.

In 1929 a young astronomer named Clyde Tombaugh began searching for the elusive ninth planet, using an observatory that Lowell had built in Flagstaff, Arizona. The only way to detect the planet was to take pairs of photographs several days apart and compare them to see if any of the faintest 'stars' had moved. Tombaugh compared the photographs using a special microscope that switched back and forth between the images. Any object that shifted position must be within the Solar System, and the further away it was, the less it would have moved.

Tombaugh first saw Pluto on these two pictures, which were taken six days apart in January 1930 at the Lowell Observatory.

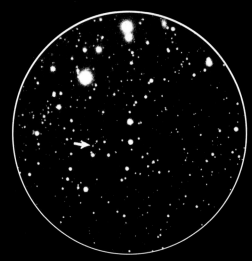

Discovering Charon

Pluto's moon Charon was discovered in 1978 by astronomer James W. Christy of the US Naval Observatory. While studying high-magnification images of Pluto, Christy noticed a bulge on one side of the planet. Other pictures soon showed that the moon orbited in a period of about 6 days, but it was not until 1994 that the Hubble Space Telescope finally produced pictures of the two separate worlds. Charon is named after the boatman who ferried dead souls across the mythical River Styx into Pluto's kingdom.

BELOW: *Pluto was named after the Greek god of the underworld, who was also known as Hades.*

Tombaugh's search could have lasted a lifetime, but he was very lucky. In February 1930 he discovered a planet on photographs taken the previous month – the tiny dot was 250 times fainter than Neptune. It was named Pluto after the Greek god of the underworld, partly in honour of Lowell, whose initials are the first two letters of Pluto.

But Pluto turned out to be too small to affect Neptune's orbit, and so for the next few decades astronomers argued over whether there was a 'Planet X' beyond Pluto. It was only in recent times that astronomers realized Neptune's puzzling orbit was caused by the inner planets. This meant that there was no need for a Planet X, although one might still exist well beyond Pluto. It also meant that Pluto's discovery was an amazing coincidence – the planet just happened to be

Probes to the outer planets

Most of our knowledge of the outer planets comes from the *Voyager 2* **space probe**. *Voyager 2* was launched from Earth in 1977 and flew towards Uranus and Neptune in a huge spiral that also took it past Jupiter and Saturn on the way. At each encounter, it used the planet's **gravity** to change course and speed up towards the next destination. Unfortunately, this meant that each planet could be studied in detail for only a few hours.

ABOVE: *This artist's impression shows Voyager 2's encounter with Neptune. The bright star in the bottom right is the Sun.*

As *Voyager 2* approached Uranus in January 1986, one of its first discoveries was the planet's strange **magnetic field**. Scientists in **mission control** were also surprised by Uranus's calm and featureless **atmosphere**. The probe took the first detailed photographs of Uranus's **rings** and took close-up pictures of the moon Miranda. It also photographed the other major moons and discovered ten small new moons.

Then it was on to Neptune, which the probe reached in August 1989. *Voyager 2* flew near Neptune's **north pole** before sweeping south to fly past Triton. On its way it discovered Neptune's strong magnetic field and several small moons, as well as Proteus, which turned out to be larger than Nereid.

*Voyager 2 discovered a hazy layer of **methane** in Neptune's upper atmosphere. The methane layer shows up red in this photograph from the probe.*

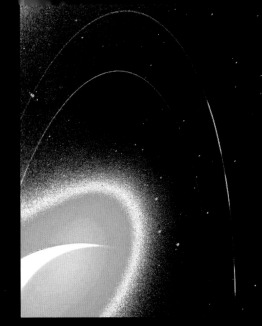

As *Voyager 2* left the Neptune system, it turned its cameras back and photographed the planet's mysterious **rings**, which were lit from behind by the Sun. Astronomers had been mystified by the fact that Neptune's rings seem to stretch only part of the way around the planet, but the probe showed that they were complete, though thicker on one side. After leaving Neptune, *Voyager 2* and its twin *Voyager 1* disappeared into the outer reaches of the Solar System. They are still flying through space today, but they are now billions of miles away from the Sun and heading towards the stars.

Voyager 2 *took the first clear pictures of Neptune's two main rings as the probe flew away from the planet.*

No space probes have yet visited Pluto, but astronomers can figure out what its surface is like by studying the colour of the light it reflects. Most theories about Pluto come from comparison with Triton, which is thought to have been similar to Pluto until it was captured and transformed by Neptune's gravity.

NASA had planned to send a small, high-speed probe to Pluto in 2004. Called the *Pluto-Kuiper Express*, it would have reached Pluto in about ten years. This **mission** is currently on hold, but scientists still hope to get a probe to Pluto by 2020. After that date Pluto's thin air will freeze as the planet enters its 200-year winter.

The Pluto-Kuiper Express *passes Pluto in this artist's impression, with Charon at bottom right.*

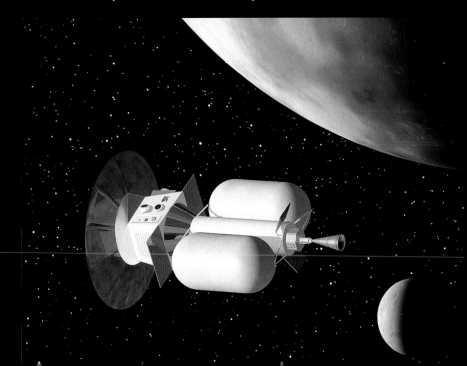

Could humans live there?

ABOVE: *This artist's impression shows a crewed spaceship visiting Pluto.*

BELOW: *Using ropes to climb and helmet lights to see their way, astronauts explore an enormous cliff on Miranda in this artist's impression. A crewed mission to Miranda is very unlikely to happen in the near future.*

You turn around at Pluto, and your ship's engines fire up again for the long journey back to Earth. It's been several decades since you left home, but you've spent most of that time asleep. As you prepare to go back into **suspended animation** for the return journey, you wonder whether humans could ever settle out here.

A human settlement near Uranus, Neptune or Pluto would need a long-term power supply. Solar energy is useless this far away from the Sun, and all the solid moons seem to have frozen **cores**, so you couldn't tap them for internal heat. But the outer Solar System is rich in the other vital requirement for settlement – water. All the water is frozen solid, but if you could melt it you could probably also split it into its chemical components to make oxygen for breathing and **hydrogen** for rocket fuel.

However, there is little reason to settle here. The outer Solar System has no resources that we cannot get more easily from the inner planets, and exploration is cheaper and safer when it's done by robotic **space probes**. Humans will probably never colonize the outer planets.

Glossary

asteroid large chunk of rock left over from when the planets formed

asteroid belt ring of asteroids that orbit the Sun between the orbits of Mars and Jupiter

astronaut person trained to go into space

atmosphere layer of gas trapped by gravity around the surface of a planet or moon

axis imaginary line through the middle of a planet or moon that it spins around

cirrus wispy clouds that form high in the sky

comet large chunk of ice that grows long, glowing tails when near the Sun

core centre of a planet, star or moon

crescent curved shape like one segment of an orange

crust solid outer surface of a planet or moon

debris fragments of rock, dust, ice or other materials

diameter width of an object measured by drawing a straight line through its centre

Edgeworth-Kuiper belt ring of comets and larger icy worlds orbiting beyond Neptune, including the planet Pluto

element chemical that cannot be split into other chemicals

ellipse stretched circle or oval

equator imaginary line around the centre of a planet or moon midway between the poles

gas giant huge planet made mostly out of gas. Jupiter, Saturn, Uranus and Neptune are all gas giants.

geyser eruption of boiling liquid or gas from underground

gravity force that pulls objects together. The heavier or closer an object is, the stronger its gravity.

Great Red Spot enormous storm on Jupiter that spins around like a hurricane

helium gas found in the Sun and in the gas giants. Helium is the second most common element in the Universe.

hydrogen simplest, lightest and most common element in the Universe. Hydrogen makes up most of the gas in the Sun and in the gas giants.

impact crater circular crater made when a comet, asteroid or meteorite hits a planet or moon

Kuiper belt object icy object in the Edgeworth-Kuiper belt. Pluto is a Kuiper belt object.

lander spacecraft that lands on a moon or planet

lava molten rock on a planet or moon's surface

magnetic field region around a planet, moon or star where a compass can detect the magnetic poles

magnetic pole point on a planet or moon that a compass points directly towards or directly away from. The magnetic poles are generally near the north and south poles.

mass measure of the amount of matter in an object. The mass of an object can be measured as weight when the object is on a planet.

meteor small piece of space rock that burns up in a planet's atmosphere, producing a streak of light called a shooting star

meteorite space rock that lands on Earth

methane gas made of the elements carbon and hydrogen. Methane is a type of organic compound.

mission expedition to visit a specific target in space, such as a planet, moon, star or comet

mission control base on Earth from which scientists monitor a spacecraft's progress

nebula vast cloud of gas and dust in outer space. Nebulas often glow in beautiful colours.

north pole point on surface of a planet or moon that coincides with the top of its axis

orbit path an object takes around another when it is trapped by the larger object's gravity; or, to take such a path

organic compound substance made up of molecules containing carbon atoms

particle tiny fragment of an atom. Particle can also mean a speck of dust or dirt.

planetesimal small, planet-like ball of debris that formed in the early Solar System

pole point on surface of a planet or moon that coincides with the top or bottom end of its axis

radar technology using short pulses of radio waves to calculate an object's position or shape

ring circle made up of millions of ice or rock particles orbiting together around a planet

rotate to turn around

rotation movement of a planet, moon or star turning around its centre, or axis

sidereal day time taken for a planet to make one complete rotation. The sidereal day is not necessarily the same length as the normal day (the time from one sunrise to the next).

south pole point on the surface of a planet or moon that coincides with the bottom end of its axis

space probe robotic vehicle sent from Earth to study the Solar System

suspended animation very deep sleep like hibernation. It is not yet possible for humans to go into suspended animation.

Books and websites

Brimner, Larry Dane. *Uranus – A True Book*. London: Franklin Watts, 1999.
Couper, Heather, and Henbest, Nigel. *The DK Space Encyclopedia.* London: Dorling Kindersley, 1999.
Englebert, Phyllis. *The Handy Space Answer Book*. London: The Gale Group, 1997.
Furniss, Tim. *The Solar System – Spinning Through Space*. London: Hodder Wayland (Hodder & Stoughton Children's Division), 1999.
nssdc.gsfc.nasa.gov/photo_gallery/ – NASA NSSDC Photo Gallery
seds.lpl.arizona.edu/nineplanets/nineplanets/nineplanets.html – Nine Planets home page
stardate.utexas.edu/resources/ssguide/ – Stardate Solar System Guide
www.enchantedlearning.com/subjects/astronomy/planets – Enchanted Learning
www.jpl.nasa.gov/ice_fire//pkexprss.htm – Pluto-Kuiper Express

Index

Picture Credits
Key: t – top, b – below, c – centre, l – left, r – right. **NASA**: 3, 4–5b, 7, 8r, 9l, 9r, 10t, 12b, 13, 16, 17, 18b, 18–19t, 19b, 20b, 20–21t, 21b, 23t, 25, 26b, 34b, 35t, JPL/California Institute of Technology 1, 2, 10b, 28–29; **SOHO***: 4l; **Alan Fitzimmons**: 29t; **Calvin J. Hamilton**: 14tl, 14tr, 14b, 15b; **Lowell Observatory**: 32b; **The Art Archive**: 33t; **Mary Evans Picture Library**: 30, 31t, 31b, 33b; **Ronald Grant Archive**: 20th Century Fox 15t; **Science Photo Library**: 32t, 35b, Julian Baum/New Scientist 36t, Chris Butler 36b, Tony Craddock 21t, Mark Garlick 12t, Claus Lunau/Foci/Bonnier Publications 24, NASA 8l, Seth Shostak 34t, Sheila Terry 11b.
Front Cover: NASA. Back Cover: NASA, JPL/California Institute of Technology.
*SOHO is a project of international cooperation between ESA & NASA.